The Red Strobe

poems by

Theta Pavis

Finishing Line Press
Georgetown, Kentucky

The Red Strobe

for Erik

Copyright © 2025 by Theta Pavis
ISBN 979-8-88838-865-5 First Edition
All rights reserved under International and Pan-American Copyright Conventions. No part of this book may be reproduced in any manner whatsoever without written permission from the publisher, except in the case of brief quotations embodied in critical articles and reviews.

ACKNOWLEDGMENTS

Grateful acknowledgment to the editors of the following journals, in which some of these poems were first published.

Pulse; "What You Were Wearing"
The Amherst Review; "Honey"
The Red Wheelbarrow; "The Forced Integration of Woodshop"; "The Beach Chronicles"
Mom Egg Review; "Thinking of Susan at the Follow-up"; "Wide Black Wale"
MER Vox Folio online; "Homework"; "Passing the Orchards"
Orgeon East; "Evidence"
Spillwords.com; "Magic Times"
The Journal of New Jersey Poets; "Driving Past the Bayway Refinery"

Special thanks to poet Dimitri Reyes—teacher, editor, inspiration.

Publisher: Leah Huete de Maines
Editor: Christen Kincaid
Cover Art: *The Red Cantilever* by Nirushi Jain
Author Photo: Pete Labrozzi
Cover Design: Diane Cuddy

Order online: www.finishinglinepress.com
also available on amazon.com

Author inquiries and mail orders:
Finishing Line Press
PO Box 1626
Georgetown, Kentucky 40324
USA

Contents

The Beach Chronicles 1
Second Opinion 2
Something About Survival 3
Drinking the Cider 4
Wide Black Wale 5
Driving Past the Bayway Refinery 6
Honey 7
The Hunters 8
The Natural World 9
Evidence 10
New Season 12
Homework 13
Thinking of Susan at the Follow-up 14
Emergence 16
Crushed 17
Things We Don't Say 19
The Red Strobe 20
The Forced Integration of Woodshop 22
Magic Times 23
Passing the Orchards 24
What You Were Wearing 25
Amniocentesis 26
C-section 27
Who is the Juggernaut? 28
Advice for Single Mothers Hanging On 29
Early Machines 30
A Kindness 32

The Beach Chronicles

She would stretch herself out on the sand
like she owned the world and the world
loved her and we loved it.

Nothing ever went wrong at the ocean.
I don't remember sunburns.
She was free there, even with four
children in tow. The water bottles were
frozen, our cooler was packed.
Her fried chicken and potato salad, covered
in paprika dust, filling the old, dented
metal bowl. There was fresh fruit for
later, peach juice dripping down our
chins and one icy, green glass Heineken
at the end of the day for her, the sun
going down. The sand castles built,
empires of the day drawn out to sea and
fallen, our books and bodies coated in sand,
our towels forever damp, the ocean, quiet
and warm. She'd pack us up for the drive
home and when they all fell asleep in the
backseat it would be just me and her,
as it had been at the beginning. I'd peel
back the plastic lid of her black coffee
and hand it to her. I'd love her despite
everything and a great satisfaction would
settle over us.

We drove back there after she died,
a box of ash closed on my lap. My hand
over the lid. A child's yellow bucket at
the ready. I waded in and set her free.

Second Opinion

In shock we pushed open that glass door
and sat in the room of rasped breath
waiting and breathing the odors of ports
punched into skin.

Waiting. Waiting for the vanguard, a
Goliath of oncology. I didn't know whether
to hate him or throw myself at his feet.

But after all the chart viewing, scan reading,
insurance wrangling, what he did was
stare into her eyes. When he told her
she would make it, my mind was a peasant

full of mistrust. Was the crust being offered rife
with mold and weevils? What he saw in her pupils
was defiance. What happened, of course,
was that she suffered. What happened was skin

and bones. What happened was her shivering so
much I climbed into her bed to hold her, to quell
the shaking. And the trembling went inside me.

Something About Survival

From my bedroom window we used to watch the old men huddle outside the synagogue, a silent Sabbath. No one on the sidewalk but them and their grey beards stark against the black coats. Their felted fedoras, like the dots at the end of so many question marks. I felt the hunch of their shoulders from across the street.

Years later I came back to find that temple turned into bespoke condos. I sat in the now-plush basement with the other new moms, watching our toddlers tumble on white carpets and all I could think of was those old men, and their women, whom we never saw.

All I could think of was the life we'd had on this street. My mother dropping my baby brother off at the sitter's apartment, handing him over that first day, the end of another maternity leave. His warm, thrush smell still on her as we walked away. Her wiping away tears. Her not meeting my eyes.

She swallowed it down. We hurried past the curvaceous stone stoops. Today I looked for signs of that long gone congregation and wished I could hear the cantor who used to call out in that synagogue across the street. Did his voice make the windows rattle? Did it send a vibration into our walkup? Did it hum, slightly, along the floorboards? Did it echo in my brother's cry?

Drinking the Cider

What made it sublime was the empty orchard.
The wheels of my father's long Ford International turning
off the two-lane road without warning, crunching up the gravel
to the very edge of the stand. No customers but us and the man
at the cider press. The afternoon burst open with smashed apple,
serendipity and a sweet, tart smell of aliveness and paring knives.

A tawny liquid gold was handed to me. We drank it straight from the jug.
The anatomy of my senses clanging with delight, the farmer's taciturn
face turned towards the back room, where the transfiguration happened,
an inflorescence of apple, the sound of the press, a feeling of red skins
on the floor, jugs of juice, amber glory like the highlights in my hair.
The joy of the first sip, then the desire to drown in it. The succulence.

My father and I smiling at each other, drunk on fall and the empty
road rollicking away towards his wooden house in the pleasing quietude
of upstate New York. The warbled song of the barn swallow so different
from my regular life in the city. Dad took a white cotton handkerchief,
a clean one always in his pocket, and wiped his lips, flush with apple
essence and the warmth of the day. His black hair and cloudy-day eyes

now shining, and me, so much a nervous copy him
but auburn like autumn and my mother. Did we know then
how much we loved each other? We carried the jugs
to the car and glided home over the rolls in the old road.

Wide Black Wale

We are moving down the corridor in slow motion
the fragile bones on your back sticking out like
the beaks of some odd bird, my sweet albatross.
My god I'd give anything to see you morph phoenix.

My legs move softly over the carpet
the wide black wale of my corduroy pants
rubbing together softly in an almost musical way.

I push your rolling IV stand with one hand
and let you lean on me with the other. We inch
towards the big window, a washed-out industrial view.

January is ending and it's the year of the horse
for both of us, born under that sign of happy
freedom, now, tethered as we are.

The bit in my mouth, uncomfortable.
Painful to ask for help.

Driving Past the Bayway Refinery

Slender spires of flange and fire, flashing lights
and broil of fume. Linden is a pungent dreamscape
on the side of the turnpike. A sprawling sci-fi city.
A whispering unknowable hiss of chemicals, invisible
benzene floating vapors heavier than air. Figures in chalk
white overalls move slowly around the snake world
of pipes. The workers climb, past fat round vats, holding
tanks so large there are spiral staircases bolted and curling
around the sides for them to scale in their steel-toed boots.
The whole place is a machine making fuel for other
machines run by humans crawling over massive drums.
In the air a skyfull of gritty plumes, a reeking system,
a wondrous menace of nitrogen oxide, carbon
monoxide, sulfur dioxide, hydrogen sulfide, leaving
behind effluvia and cancer, the price per gallon.
The chemical pink of a New Jersey sunset.

Honey

When my mother was seven
her friends disturbed a hive.

The bees chased the children.
The children chased for home,
stingers covering their new skin.

But my mother stood
still like stone.

Her unmovable body
an amber core.

The bees covered her,
tried to enter her mouth, eyes.

When the last one flew away,
she walked home, calmly, without a sting.

She did not remember to stay still
like that, later, with men.

The Hunters

Before she knocked on the door
my mother would line the three of us up:
the flesh, the blood, the bone.

We climbed the stairs behind her,
me holding the doughy, just rising hands
of my little brother and sister. It was August.

By the time we reached the landing
the children's black curls would be
rolling even tighter in the humidity.

Sweat blistered my upper lip.
The hallways were always dark but
we could make out the faces

of the landlord or super, staring
down at the damp lot of us, alone with
one woman to carry it all.

They didn't want us. They never did.
Our mother smiled. Our own mouths
formed small worried lines.

The first place that finally took us was
on Prospect Street, where we were
robbed one day when everyone was out.

They took the little television and
the stereo. We had no jewels but ourselves.

The Natural World

When I was a girl they
took me to the country.
Fire ants burned
my legs and yellow jackets
stung my arms but
nothing left a mark like you.

You raised my flowered night
gown and rubbed my 8-year-old
body like it was a genie's lamp
and wishes would come out of me.

Your sandpaper hands.

What surprised me most
was not that you did it,
but that you brought along a
chair to sit by my bedside
so you would be more comfortable.

That my infant sister in her
crib did not wake up,
and that when I woke, I feigned
a stirring that made you
leave, backing out of the room
with the chair in your hands.

Like a lion tamer, no whip in your hand
but the one you left in my mind.

Evidence

When the store detective
caught me in aisle six
I was up to my elbow
in Froot Loops,
desperately fishing for
the plastic toy of the month.

He sidled up to me,
a smirk on his greasy face.
I froze, fingers just skimming
the plastic wrapper, buried
beneath the sweet loops, small
wreaths of red, yellow, orange.

One aisle over
we found my mother,
the triumphant detective
and me, shamefaced pillager
of cereal boxes.

The offered evidence,
the defiled box—with
Toucan Sam's beak open
in amazement—
was held above me.

My small, brown-haired head
and pale face turned down
to stare at the ShopRite floor.

Then my mother took the box.
Like this is what we ate
every single day for breakfast,
and tossed it into our cart.

Like the store cop
could drop dead.

And though he followed us
all the way to checkout,
she never flinched.

New Season

Winter's ice has broken the terracotta
pots that sat in the backyard and finally
destroyed your half-barrel planter,
the one with the sage that grew
out of control, its shriveled leaves,
once soft and long, cling to dead sticks.

I watch the wood that's splintered.

I sit in the sun and lift my face, the way you did.
Nearby, early daffodils raise their fragile
perennial heads, oblivious to your absence.
I stare at the small yellow coronas, six little petals.

It's almost unbearable.

I imagine the gardener I will call
to help me—what will she say
about the short logs surrounding the
little plot with the crocus you planted?

How can I tell her you buried all the family's
cats here and that it cannot be disturbed?

It seems we could have just
put you ashes here, instead
of in the ocean as requested.

My daughter is collecting the dead
brown leaves from the oak tree you
tended and she's trying on the now too
small gardening gloves you bought her—
she's longing for the spade without knowing
she's longing for your hand on the handle.

Homework

My daughter studies Latin at the kitchen table.
Cornelius is in a ditch once more, his wagon wheel
undone on some Roman road. On the black
and white page, his consort Lavinia raises clasped hands.

"They've been traveling all marking period!"
my daughter says, exasperated. I quiz her when she asks,
my butchered phrasing makes her laugh. A five-paragraph
essay on a book I've never read lays to the side waiting.
Sheets of music drift to the floor; her instrument

sits by the door. There's a small pencil turned in a plastic
sharpener, with a tiny silver blade. Math is scratched upon
the page, figures I have long forgot. Formulas I can't decipher.
Like how we used to be three but one was subtracted.

Later, calligraphic mysteries of Japanese fill her notebook
with simple squares for each Kanji character to fit inside,
like a face in a window. Delicate, she wields the black pen.
I love the path she is making for herself, prisms refracting
crystal softness, shining towards her clarity. Words swirl
inside my daughter, secret unknowable languages

I cannot speak. The mouth that once looked to me
for everything now moves its lips in silent practice.
What's left out are the words she will not say
about her father, the missing man at the table.

Thinking of Susan at the Follow-up

On the black film
the picture of my breast
looks like the moon
before men landed there.

The doctor's white gloves
pinch the edge of the
black rectangle,
touching the map of me.

I am staring at the breast-crusher
in the corner, wondering who
decided to name it Selena?

What if you came here and
your name was Selena?

Or what if your cousin Susan died
when you were just a girl
and you were there, at the edge
of her bed, when it happened.

Would you stand over
the heating vent in the floor
the next morning,
watching your nightgown poof out
from the forced air?

What if that Vermont winter was
so cold the icicles outside were
as long as spears and you wanted
to break one off and take it with you?

What if your cousin died on
her birthday? And your father
didn't know what to do with the

red woolen blanket he'd bought
for a present.

So he gave it to you.

Emergence

The nurses have her up on
the tilt board when I walk in.

My sister—strapped in place.
Like a little Frankenstein,
held tight against the board,
belts across her head and wrists and legs.

Suspended, she will not take a step
or open the present I have brought her.
In this special ward, she is a
candidate for coma emergence.

Specialists will come and go, but in the end
they resort to this:
strapping her small body to a board every day,
raising her from horizontal to vertical.
Sending her system a message to wake up.

And yes, she has cracked
one soft eyelid, just a sliver
and I realize that if I crouch at her feet
and look up, I can see just a little
bit, beneath her black lash,
the shining, brown marble of her eye.

Shocking to see that brown,
so familiar, but almost like I'd
already forgotten it. That warm brown of the sun.

I recognize the eye,
small solider sent to scout the world
from the far away asteroid where she is,
checking to see if this is an afterlife.

I stay at her feet.

Crushed

Our mother mashes the peach
with a plastic fork. We slit it
open as best we could.

She's merciless, pushing the tines
through the ripe flesh, making it
succumb. Juicy rivers run.

Pressed, the pulp gives in. Smashed
the fragrance fills your room.
Life blooms despite the Purell-filled air,
closed hospital windows, bleached sheets.

Everything becomes peach.
From the one window the guilty sun
streaks onto the yellow orange mash
—glorious goo. The pit long discarded.

We are down now to the basics.
Four girls and one peach.
I hold my baby daughter on my hip
bouncing her slightly.

My mouth fills with saliva.
Still, our mother pummels the peach,
small starburst of summer.

You sit in your wheelchair, sister,
black hair, black eyes, sad
scars, some still pink, others silver.

Our mother's voice fills your room.
We are far from the farmer's market.
Far from a father's baritone love.

Our mother loves the peach
the whole, round terrible
perfection of everything.

She spoons it into your mouth,
cooing her song.
Spins to the baby,
slides it into her little oval oh.
Everyone is sustained
but there is no peach
for the mothers;
we take only air and salt.

She will not take a bite.
I will not have a taste.
No one chokes
and the plate goes clean.

Things We Don't Say

When the stranger shoved his finger inside me
air from my small lungs escaped into the stairwell,
floating over the dirty tile.

How to recapture that lost breath? Did it travel
up the stairs towards my mother or is it still
trapped inside those long hallways?

Near the window of my old bedroom
the fire escape was bolted to the bricks.
It's still up there.

Once we stood on it
to watch the total eclipse.

The world slowly darkened.
Remember: a metallic taste rose
in my mouth.

It returns sometimes
without warning.

The Red Strobe

One moment alone in the neighbor's kitchen.
A foot on the linoleum, then the clack of the dog's
nails near his dish.

When the neighbor's dog bites, the scene ends.
Outside it's all barren lots and the spot
where you buried the dead kitten in
your father's empty box of checkbooks.

You'll limp back home with your jeans torn open.
Even that small, your skin released particles of fear
and it was never a smell that attracted a barrier.
There is no sheath.

At home with your father, a fever is burning.
You'll be placed in ice water, in a
deep white tub. There's your favorite pink plastic soap
dish, shaped like a hippopotamus. You stare at
the hippo's smile, shaking till your teeth clatter.

Your mind will remember the dark of that night,
broken by the red strobe of the ambulance, sweeping
over East Orange, New Jersey.
The cold metal of the emergency room table.

Something is tearing again.
Your father is standing on a dock of rotted wood
jutting into the soft lake. He's moved to the country.

He's posted a warning sign and walked you right past it,
hands full of fish hooks.

You'll fall through the splintered wood,
grey and cracking with age.
One old nail finds the skin of your hip.
Then iodine is a song, a smear on your body.

These people will save your life
but it's always after the fact.
They cannot stop the scars from collecting.

Your job is to love the scars.
Pretend they are birthmarks.
Touch them.
This one is on your hand.

Your mother named the cat Mala.
Your brother named his dog Devil.
This time Devil leaves a perfect puncture
wound on your hand.

His jaws unclamp.
You marvel at the divot.
You hardly feel a thing.

The Forced Integration of Woodshop

Mr. Halstead's gold chain bracelet glowed
in the amber dim of his basement workshop

in the cozy gloaming
his man hands, and hairy wrist, and glinting gold.

His lair of sawdust and leather invaded by us:
The girls. We sat silent on narrow benches while

he told us he didn't agree—would rather see us
upstairs in home ec, making mini-pizzas and sewing.

But he would teach us anyway because
they were making him. Everyone was rapt
and the boys, smug, sat up straighter.

But how I loved the table saw, the beveling,
the lathe and the small flock of wooden geese
we made, staining them in darker and darker
hues, then shellacking them, then
watching them sail, shiny, across my father's wall.

Each year Halstead led his students through the same routine—
a decorative cutting board for mom, the geese for dad.

You stood to grip the saws and marvel at the various teeth,
you stood to push the wood towards the unforgiving bite.

Magic Times

When you dressed me as Cleopatra
I won the costume contest,
standing on the school stage, draped in royal
purple polyester, surveying my subjects,
a tinfoil crown on my head,
embellished with a small silver snake
shining over my hair. You knew flair.

I was a gypsy girl in dime store gold,
a cowgirl in faux and fringed buckskin,
Princess Leia loose in velvet folds of white,
brown yarn hair buns coiled and
set in place with secret bobby pins.

I was a robot with working lights,
I was a witch, I was a ghost, I was your girl.
I could be anything. You made
life fun sometimes. You made it
magic. You made the number
seven in M&M's on my chocolate
cake. Mama you could be so sweet.

Passing the Orchards

Driving back from you, I pass silent through blanched winter
landscapes. It's late. The bare apple trees seem angry, their
spindly branches raise bristling fists into the grey afternoon sky.

I know they'll blossom and it will be a miracle. I try to see us in
the future, slowly struggling through the grassy lane at some farm,
a bag of apples in one hand, your walker making ruts in the
green earth.

Like pie crust and cold butter, I want to be that person with her hands
in the dough, working it and making it mine. Laying each slice down
for the oven's warmth, the succulence of life.

I imagine a bright kitchen, an orchard, the highway, is a place to get
to and must be better than rolling my eyes to the past, to the rearview
mirror I love, so fiercely, all the time.

I'm moving through the present in the slow lane, letting the cars pass
me, but the present is still a place I struggle with. I visit, I kiss your
cheek, I try to stay calm when you get frustrated. But there seems no
place to lay down my grief.

I've tucked it in the trunk.
It comes with me everywhere.

What You Were Wearing

They handed me your clothes,
the winter boots,
the dark folded jeans in their
impossible size 5.

I put them in my trunk, then
drove around for weeks
orbiting your hospital like
a satellite sister.

Every time I had to open
the trunk, loading in the
groceries, the rock salt,
someone's suitcase,
your clothes were waiting for me.

I stood in parking lots, the hatchback
of my car open like a mouth and
my mouth open like a hatch.

The brass buckle
on your leather belt still
burning like a sun.

Amniocentesis

The amniotic sac, that
portable sea-sack within.
Unseen sea, wet and
globular. Your private tidal

basin, wet estuary with
hope and salt, private ocean
after ocean wave, drifting you
in the confines of body, waving
fingers finding ocean's mouth.

Next week the doctor wants
to guide the needle in. The
doctor's face says needle.

But I wonder what your
face will say in the secret
wonder sea. Will you think
the tide's gone out? Will
you head for shore?

C-section

The doctor's name was Gross
and when he said "cut" we could
hear his tongue hit the front of his teeth.

So precise. Like the scalpel
slicing through the abdominal wall
and all the things I'd planned.

Here the belly flesh has offered its
protest and won't lay pretty.
It's marked by an undulating scar.

This snaking making its way
below the stomach
and between the hips.

This crooked smile above the pubic bone.
This purposeful mark.
Like a line drawn in the sand.

Like the lined-up men must have
looked from a distance, marching
as they were, behind their general
towards Gaul.

The gall of it all.

Because now, when they ask,
I am forced to repeat Caesar's name first,
instead of yours.

Who is the Juggernaut?

At the laser tag birthday party my daughter says she was handed a fake gun that weighed seven pounds. Her voice is raspy from running, her hair tangled with sweat. She climbs into the car and guzzles water. Her team chose her, she says to be the juggernaut.

Meaning they had to protect her. They ran, a pack of teenage girls, gaming in the dark, shooting light beams at each other. We pull out of the lot and she's flush with excitement and cake, and I think—I want to protect this girl, who is so close now to leaving home. What things will be aiming for her out in this world? I don't want to let her go, this bright, agile being.

But of course I will. And we are already unspooling. In her room I smell mall-bought perfume, warm spiced vanilla. Her kiwi scented lotion. Her strawberry lip gloss. Her floor heaped with dirty clothes and books. Her unvacuumed rug where the cat curled in a sun patch.

After she is in bed, I look up the rules of laser tag, learning she was the target of the game. I consider our perspectives—she saw her friends running to shield her. I saw the target they put on her back. I can't help but think to when I was the daughter and my existence was a juggernaut in my mother's marriage. I was the unstoppable force simply by existing. A problem with my breathing and growing and the tangles in my hair.

But here in the present I have made my girl a nexus, not a problem. I let her hair grow any way she wants it, pixie to mop. Tangle to curl. I let her grow anyway she wants, near to far.

Advice for Single Mothers Hanging On

Be like the ivy,
climbing the wall
along the old red brick.
Spread yourself out, curve
around windows. You, a green
tendril sometimes peeking into
other lives. Be in gratitude for the
lovers glimpsed inside, despite your solitary
days spent clinging to the building of life. Time
spent working to stay tethered, to feel sunshine
and rain come down, rainbow shards passing through you.

Be
like the ivy,
vigorous and
threaded to all
the other vines,
you with friends so
great they will help chisel
cracks even into hardest stone.
Don't look down, look up, cloud dancer.
Smell the river below, moisture mixing with
the exhaust of the cars pulsing far beneath. Be
verdant, strong, tenacious. Feast and grow from the
simplest things: photosynthesis, windowsills, words spoken
out loud, secrets repeated, stories unspooled. Remember the
precious relics waiting for you: recipes, record players, the soft
silver frame holding the old black and white photo. Rejoice at the
star called the sun, the seal in the harbor, the child holding the balloon by
its string. When she lets go, you'll hear a sharp cry and the bright red orb
will drift quickly past you, so green and dappled, where at last you belong,
to yourself.

Early Machines

Your smell heightens, then your taste.
The knobby balls of your spine climb up
your back, each orb a small planet I touch.

A tube moves in and out as you breathe.
Like a tendril, reaching for something I can't give.
Your mouth gasps, your gums glare.
The nearly naked pubic mound exposed.

Your numbers, the formula of my life.
Your fevers, a math problem climbing
with no solution. You burn.

Your bile backs up, a dark primordial green
seeping ooze, the color of an ancient slime we
think we've crawled out of

but it lives on in us, coursing—propelled
from the gallbladder into the bile duct making its way
to the liver. A well traveled pathway of waste.

Your tumor exposed a frailty in the system.
I drain your bile, pour it into the toilet,
dump the vomit from the plastic bin in after it.

You throw up in bed, at the picnic table, over the sink.
It's sinking in. You are a being of bile. An essential
creature, sallow, tired, the jaundice crept in and surprised us.

Just a tinge in the eyes, before your skin turned yellow
and your piss an orange last seen in the Paleozoic period,
in a sunset that burned before humans existed.

The body is an early machine with fire dancing in the limbs.

Your oldest child, the one with the weakest stomach
cleans the puke, flushes the line, wipes the brow, swabs
the decks, shakes the sterile saline, peels the bandages.

Your arms sag with lost muscle tone
and the skin has lines running down it now
like paper I could write on.

A Kindness

Hard-crusted morning. February's a hangover of sleet.
I stomp forward, punch my feet through
the frozen snow swept against my car.

It's almost up to my knees, all I have to do
is unlock the frozen door. Coax the old motor to turn
over. Try to feel the weak sun glistening off the ice.

Then go back inside and get my mother. Go back
and get my wry and vanishing mother and help her
over the slick drifts and into a warm car. Push through

the Lincoln Tunnel, before barreling up the West Side Highway
and the crosstown grid. Just to walk her into that hospital, again, for

radiation. The coffee is made, paperwork packed. That's all I have
to do. Pry open the car's frozen door, scrape the windshield clean.
Turn the ignition.

But the keys slip from my gloved hands into the blanched furrows
surrounding the car. They disappear, quicksilver, quietly
slipping into white.

The keys gone, and now all I have to do is find them with my hands
dredging the snow, digging, up to my elbows and—nothing.

The keys are lost in the white and I could almost, at that moment, be
the arctic explorer lost in a vast blank, the sled dogs long gone.

The street is silent. Each breath I gasp in comes out visible and impotent.
I am numb and not from cold—stuporous. Then the neighbor, who
always walks his happy dog down our block comes along and sees me

frozen there. Flaky crystals melting over the rim of my boots and he stops
to ask what is wrong. And I don't say cancer is killing her and I want to die

and I don't say divorce moved into my house and I don't
say I secretly have a pack of cigarettes in my pocket and I don't

say how can it still be winter? I say—I've dropped my keys in the snow,
and he stops with his black dog and plunges his arms into the white piles

and finds them.
And I have never been more grateful in my life.

Theta Pavis is a writer and educator. Her poems have appeared in *The Journal of New Jersey Poets, The Red Wheelbarrow, Mom Egg Review, Spillwords Press, Why to These Rocks: 50 Years of Poetry from the Community of Writers* (HeyDay Books), and many others. A collection of her poetry was shortlisted in 2022 by Yellow Arrow Publishing. She was longlisted for the 2022 Emerging Poet Prize from *Palette Poetry*. Her work has been performed onstage by Poetry Well in New York and she has received residencies from Arts By The People (New Jersey) and Bethany Arts Community (New York).

For nearly a decade she was the Director of Student Media at New Jersey City University where her students won numerous awards. In 2021, the Society of Professional Journalists (NJ chapter) named her "Journalism Educator of the Year." She has taught at UCLA, Kean University, the University of the Arts, St. Peter's University and NJCU. Most recently she led media workshops for students at Rutgers-Newark.

As a reporter, Theta worked for daily newspapers in Pennsylvania and New York. She was the founding editor of *Palisade* magazine and has freelanced for numerous outlets, including *Consumer Reports* and *Wired.com*.

Theta has a master's degree from the Columbia University Graduate School of Journalism and has also worked with numerous nonprofits, including Sociologists for Women in Society. She's committed to social justice and issues of diversity and inclusion. She lives in Jersey City, NJ.

www.thetapavis.com

www.ingramcontent.com/pod-product-compliance
Lightning Source LLC
Chambersburg PA
CBHW022046080426
42734CB00009B/1260